UNWRAPPING ADVENT'S GIFTS

Susan L Klein

A Note from the Author

Advent has always been a favorite time for me. The tradition of a wreath and candles has not only been in my church but in my home, too. A few years ago I realized I was saying the right words when I lit the candles, but I didn't focus on what they meant.

In my research about the Advent candle tradition I've found it varies among denominations. The most common themes are Hope, Love, Joy and Peace but not always in the same order. If I've written them in a different order than your tradition, you can read this book in the order of your own tradition. I also learned historically the first two weeks of Advent focused on looking forward to Christ's second coming while the last two weeks of Advent focused on Christ's birth. I've written this book to honor that tradition. Candle color is another varying tradition among denominations and cultures.

It is my prayer that your faith is enriched as you read and study and that your greatest Christmas present be the One God sent.

Wrapped in God's love and tenderly sent with His only Son are God's gifts to each of us this Advent season. With a clear, victorious vision of the future and a wonderous look at the past, we are securely in the center of the promise Jesus holds. As we light our Advent candles and focus on Jesus's promised second coming and then the miracle of His birth, we are invited to receive much more than the presents under our trees. The Advent gifts He has given need only to be unwrapped and accepted.

HOPE

THE DISCIPLES' GIFT

Acts 1:9-11

> *After he said this, he was taken up before their very eyes, and a cloud hid him from their sight. They were looking intently up into the sky as he was going, when suddenly two men dressed in white stood beside them. "Men of Galilee," they said, "why do you stand here looking into the sky? This same Jesus, who has been taken from you into heaven, will come back in the same way you have seen him go into heaven."*

Did the disciples feel hope in that moment or despair? The kingdom of Jesus was not what they expected. In Mark 10:35-40, two disciples ask Jesus for the right to sit beside him in his kingdom. They didn't understand. They expected an earthly kingdom. In Matthew 16:21-23 after Jesus explains to his disciples all he will endure in Jerusalem, Peter rebukes Jesus saying, "This shall never happen to you." He didn't understand. Jesus had to die before he sat on his throne. Peter could not see beyond death. Jesus explains to him, "...you do not have in mind the things of God, but the things of men." After Jesus told his disciples more than once he would be raised after three days in the tomb, they weren't watching for that to happen. They were not at the tomb on the third day expecting the resurrection. Luke explains clearly in Luke 18:34, "The disciples did not understand any of this. Its meaning was hidden from them, and they did not know what he was talking about." Even at the Great Commission in Matthew 28:16-20 when Jesus directed his disciples to go out to every nation, teach his commands, and baptize in the name of the trinity making disciples for Jesus now that he is in his kingdom, some doubted. After 40 days with Jesus appearing to them on earth even after his death and resurrection, did they now understand his kingdom was a heavenly one? Had their crushed expectations been turned to hope, the hope of doing his work and joining him in heaven one day?

Before his ascension, Jesus appeared to his disciples. Luke 2:45-49 tells us Jesus "opened their minds so they could understand the Scriptures." Then he directed them to stay in the city until they received the gift God had promised: the gift of the Holy Spirit. As Jesus ascended, were the disciples able to use their new understanding to see beyond death now, to experience the great hope of an eternity in heaven with Jesus?

The reality was that Jesus was not dead. Hope and expectation were what was left. The emptiness they felt at Jesus's death was filled with the Holy Spirit. Despair dissolved by hope. The disciples had to untangle their experiences and their memories and all Jesus taught them so they could begin to get the world ready for his second coming, fulfilling the Great Commission and sharing the hope they received.

We have that same hope. The gift is ours, too. We have received the same gift of the same Holy Spirit. We, too, share the hope of an eternity in heaven with Jesus. The Holy Spirit is called a counselor, a helper, the Spirit of Truth, a guarantee of what is to come and a seal. This gift sustains us. This gift guides us. Once we've received the gift, the Holy Spirit is always present, always available. Hope is always present.

Advent is a time of renewing our focus on the hope that will fill our emptiness. Our lives become tangled in everyday worldly things. We're pulled from every direction with so many demands and responsibilities. It's difficult to keep our focus on God's path with so many distractions and sometimes disappointments. We are drained. Despair comes easily. But, with the Holy Spirit, hope wins.

During this first week of Advent we renew that hope in our own lives. Remembering the promise of heaven, we refocus our lives to reflect that hope and our Savior. We can let go of past struggles and despair and let the Holy Spirit fill our hearts with the hope Jesus offers. Just like the disciples, we need to untangle our experiences and memories, leave our past expectations in the past, and look for what God has planned for our future. His Holy Spirit will guide us and lead us to eternity with Jesus.

2 Corinthians 5:5

Now it is God who has made us for this very purpose and has given us the Spirit as a deposit, guaranteeing what is to come.

THE GIFT IN HEAVEN

1 Peter 1:3-5

> *Praise be to the God and Father of our Lord Jesus Christ! In his great mercy he has given us new birth into a living hope through the resurrection of Jesus Christ from the dead and into an inheritance that can never perish, spoil or fade – kept in heaven for you, who through faith are shielded by God's power until the coming of the salvation that is ready to be revealed in the last time.*

"Praise be!" Peter's excitement resounds in this verse. God's great mercy has given us a new birth, an adoption into the family of Christians whose lives can be saturated by the living hope of Jesus. A hope that never fades. We are given an inheritance, a piece of God's kingdom as his children, and the splendor of that inheritance will never go away. That precious gift is kept in heaven waiting for each of us who has accepted it and lived through our faith. As we wait to claim our inheritance, we are shielded by God's power until Jesus comes for us.

Peter's proclamation is a truth he wants every Christian to understand and embrace. His voice does not falter. Peter was a fisherman by trade. Fishermen were known to be rather boisterous in those days with quick tempers. As a disciple, Peter was one of the first to follow Jesus and a natural leader. He was bold and sometimes outspoken. It was Peter who rebuked Jesus and, in Matthew 16:23, caused Jesus to respond, "Get behind me, Satan!" And it was Peter who asked Jesus, "Lord, how many times shall I forgive my brother when he sins against me? Up to seven times?" (Matthew 18:21) A strong man by the demands of his trade, Peter preferred to rely on his own physical strength. In the garden, at the time of Jesus's arrest, it was Peter who drew his sword and cut off the ear of the high priest's servant in John 18:10. Bold and confident, yet Peter experienced doubt and fear. In Matthew 14:25-31, Jesus approaches the disciples' boat walking on water. Peter challenges Jesus to prove his identity. He calls Peter to come out to him on the water. Peter leaves the boat and is walking to Jesus on the waves when his fears take over, and he begins to sink. He wanted proof. Yet, thirty years later he proclaims something he cannot prove, yet believes with his whole being. The gift of an inheritance.

A gift waiting in heaven for each of us. An inheritance that is eternal. It cannot perish, it is permanent. It cannot spoil, its worth remains. It cannot fade, it is brilliant. The gift is already ours because we each belong in the family of God. We have been adopted into the living hope of Jesus. The hope that also never fades, spoils or perishes. Praise can be our only response. We have done nothing to deserve such a gift, yet, it waits for us.

As we wait for Jesus and our inheritance, do we reflect that hope? Are we living as sons and daughters of the eternal living King? Imagine the splendor of your inheritance in heaven. Earth's riches dim in comparison. Are we focused on the right riches?

Until Jesus comes again and takes us home, God's power shields us through our faith. Choosing the gift of inheritance asks us to live our faith in this broken world trusting God's power to shield us from Satan's destruction. That doesn't mean we won't be under attack. We wouldn't need a shield if there were no arrows. Like Peter, we have doubt and fear whether we are bold and outspoken or quiet and demure. However, we have hope!

Advent reminds us of God's future plans for us in heaven with Him. Jesus waits for us to join him as we wait for him to come get us. The timing is God's alone. Until that time, the gift of an inheritance is kept secure for each of us. Let's let the earthly riches dim this week as we reflect the hope of our inheritance in heaven.

Hebrews 6:19a

> *We have this hope as an anchor for the soul, firm and secure.*

A GIFT OF BELONGING

Phillipians 3:20-21

> *But our citizenship is in heaven. And we eagerly await a Savior from there, the Lord Jesus Christ, who by the power that enables him to bring everything under his control, will transform our lowly bodies so that they will be like his glorious body.*

We belong. Heaven is our home. We wait on earth for Jesus to come exchange our earthly bodies into heavenly ones and welcome us home. Hope.

The apostle Paul wrote in his second letter to the Corinthians 5:1, “Now we know that if the earthly tent we live in is destroyed, we have a building from God, an eternal house in heaven, not built by human hands.” God has already made a place for us, and it is eternal. The verses tell us this gift, the gift of citizenship, is already ours. We wait for Jesus to come for us, but our citizenship is already established. Citizenship means having the rights, privileges and duties of a citizen, membership in a community along with the protection of that community. We have heaven's protection. We have rights, privileges and duties of heaven. We should conduct ourselves as heavenly citizens. We have the privilege of calling on our heavenly Father at any time. We have membership in heaven. Paul explains further in Ephesians 2:19-20, "Consequently, you are no longer foreigners and aliens, but fellow citizens with God's people and members of God's household, built on the foundation of the apostles and prophets with Christ Jesus himself as the chief cornerstone." We are fellow citizens with not only those Christians we know now on earth, but with all of God's people. We are citizens with Moses and Aaron, Rebekah and Sarah, Job and Isaiah. And, Jesus is our cornerstone. We will be safe. We will be secure. We will be together with God's people in God's heaven. When the Hope of Heaven comes down and leads us all home, we will not be foreigners but fellow citizens together for God's glory.

The disciples tell us, too, of our citizenship. John 15:19 tells us, "If you belonged to the world, it would love you as its own. As it is, you do not belong to the world, but I have chosen you out of the world. That is why the world hates you." Chosen. Each single one of us is chosen. Once God has chosen us out of the world, living through our faith, we reflect our heavenly rights, privileges and duties allowing the riches of the world to fade. The glories of heaven magnified instead. Even our earthly bodies will become heavenly by the power of Jesus as he takes control. The tremendous beauty we will experience is unimaginable. The world hates us because the world loses control of us. We love instead of hate. We build others up instead of crushing them under our feet. We share what we have, glorifying God. In Matthew 6:19-21, we are warned not to store up earthly treasures but heavenly ones where our treasures are safe eternally. Eternal treasures only in heaven. Luke 18:22 tells of Jesus asking a man to sell everything he has and give to the poor to have treasure in heaven. What we have on earth isn't ours to keep. What we have on earth won't last. Heaven is our destination. There are the treasures we will keep.

This advent week we remind ourselves of what we already know. We have an inheritance in heaven waiting for us. We have the Holy Spirit guiding us there. And, we have citizenship with the rights, privileges, duties and protections of heaven. Colossians 3:15 gives us direction as we wait, "Let the peace of Christ rule in your hearts, since as members of one body you were called to peace. And be thankful." Hope in eternal life with Jesus, and the expectation of Jesus returning for us gives us peace. Our response is thankful praise.

Romans 8:24-25

> *For in this hope we were saved. But hope that is seen is not hope at all. Who hopes for what he already has? But if we hope for what we do not yet have, we wait for it patiently.*

A SHEPHERD'S GIFT

1 Peter 5:4

And when the Chief Shepherd appears, you will receive the crown of glory that will never fade away.

A shepherd, one of the lowliest professions in Biblical times, and a crown of glory, for royalty, describe our hope at advent. When the Chief Shepherd, Jesus, appears, we each hope to receive a crown of glory designating us as royal heirs belonging to God's kingdom forever and ever.

When Peter penned this letter, he was writing to encourage believers, specifically elders and young men in 1 Peter 5:1-10. He encourages the elders saying, "Be shepherds of God's flock that is under your care..." He calls them overseers and examples to all Christian people. He continues addressing the young men instructing them to be submissive to those who are older and to be humble. The crown of glory is the gift they look forward to as they grow to shepherd God's flock throughout their earthly lives.

At Jesus's birth the angels appeared to shepherds. Shepherds were among the first to see the baby. Shepherds were given the honor and privilege to spread the good news about the newborn savior. Lowly, yet significant. Prophets from the Old Testament times describe shepherds in detail. Isaiah paints a loving, caring and responsible picture of a shepherd in Isaiah 40:11. In his description a shepherd "gathers lambs in his arms" using his own strength when they are young and weak. He comforts them with his own strong heartbeat when he "carries them close to his heart." And, when he "gently leads those that have young," he is nurturing those who nurture others. Jeremiah 31:10 tells us a shepherd watches over the flock. A good shepherd has his entire flock in his care and keeps his watchful eye on each of them. Ezekiel offers a much richer description in Ezekiel 34:12 when he describes a shepherd who searches for his sheep and looks after them, tends them and binds the injured, searches for the lost, rescues them and brings them home, strengthens the weak, makes them rest and destroys those who are sleek and strong, threatening the safety of the whole flock. Shepherds are the caretakers.

Peter understood God's people need caretakers. In his letter to the elders, Peter is reminding the older, wiser men of their heavenly duty to the younger. The younger men need examples. They haven't lived through as much in their lifetimes and are not as wise as the older ones. He also asks the younger to learn from the older so they, too, can learn to shepherd the flock. They are cautioned not to be too proud therefore not learning in humility from the older men. They will be the older and wiser shepherds one day themselves.

Jesus used a shepherd in many of his teachings. In Matthew 9:36, Jesus feels compassion for the crowds who came to him for healing because they were "like sheep without a shepherd." Jesus calls himself a good shepherd in John 10:14 saying, "I know my sheep and my sheep know me." Jesus was willing to be a shepherd to his flock.

Are we willing to be a shepherd to God's flock? Tending God's flock is a heavenly privilege. And it is ours. Like Isaiah's shepherd, we can use our own strength to help those younger and weaker than ourselves. We can comfort and nurture them. We can watch over our flock like Jeremiah's shepherd. We can strive to be like Ezekiel's shepherd searching, rescuing, tending, strengthening and providing rest for the weary. Our flock may be small. It may be large. God has given us each a flock and asks us to faithfully shepherd them for Him. God knows how many we can handle, and He knows the gifts He has given us to share with our flock. The gift He offers us in return is a crown of glory. As we wait in hopeful expectation for Jesus to come again, our flock needs us. As we gently tend them, we will reveal the hope we have especially during the Advent season, and we can lead them home to heaven. Our crown awaits.

1 Peter 3:15

But in your hearts set apart Christ as Lord. Always be prepared to give an answer to everyone who asks you to give the reason for the hope that you have. But do this with gentleness and respect.

THE GIFT JESUS BRINGS

1 Thessalonians 2:19-20

> *"For what is our hope, our joy, or the crown in which we will glory in the presence of our Lord Jesus when he comes? Is it not you? Indeed, you are our glory and joy."*

Paul's words to the Thessalonian believers must've been like the cool shade of a tree on a blistering hot day. Through riots and opposition, they had persevered and grown in their faith. They sought to live as Christians even in a hostile culture. They needed those words of encouragement as a respite as they continued their Christian journey.

Paul realized how vital encouragement among believers is to their faith. In his letter to the Romans 1:11-12, he includes himself in that need saying, "I long to see you so that I may impart to you some spiritual gift to make you strong – that is, that you and I may be mutually encouraged by each other's faith." Mutual encouragement strengthens. Luke tells a story in Acts 15:22-35 of the church in Antioch being troubled and the council in Jerusalem sending Judas and Silas to encourage and strengthen them. Hebrews 3:13 instructs Christian people to "encourage one another daily, as long as it is called Today, so that none of you may be hardened by sin's deceitfulness." Continual encouragement, not only in times of trouble, can guard against unintentional slips into sinful behavior. Hebrews 10:25 offers this plea, "Let us not give up meeting together... but let us encourage one another..."

Together. These verses call for action together. Together we help each other nourish our faith. Together we watch for the traps and the pitfalls and pull each other out of them. Together we cannot be selfish. Hope is not selfish. Joy is not selfish. We cannot keep glory, joy and hope inside ourselves, they are from the fellowship and encouragement of others, and they radiate from all Christian lives. The hope of Advent is not about our own personal salvation but all of us together. On the day Jesus comes, we will be caught up in the clouds with him together to go home to heaven. It is in that moment when we receive our crown and experience the fullness of hope. Glory and hope will be fully realized only in the presence of Jesus and all believers on that day he comes. The presence of Jesus is the gift that brings the fullness of hope, joy and glory. The presence of Jesus is the gift.

Hope. Hope in the second coming of Jesus includes all Christian people. As we focus on our own faith we must focus outward to receive the best of the gifts. Our glory and joy in Jesus's presence will radiate from those we have been caught up to heaven with and their glory and joy will radiate from us.

We can refocus our hope on earth to reflect that heavenly hope by focusing outward on our brothers and sisters. Allow hope in Jesus to radiate from your life to everyone who is watching. Those encouraged by you will be your glory and joy in heaven.

1 Thessalonians 4:13-18

> *Brothers, we do not want you to be ignorant about those who fall asleep, or to grieve like the rest of men who have no hope. We believe that Jesus died and rose again and so we believe that God will bring with Jesus those who have fallen asleep in him. According to the Lord's own word, we tell you that we who are still alive, who are left till the coming of the Lord, will certainly not precede those who have fallen asleep. For the Lord himself will come down from heaven, with a loud command, with the voice of the archangel and with the trumpet call of God, and the dead in Christ will rise first. After that, we who are still alive and are left will be caught up together with them in the clouds to meet the Lord in the air. And so we will be with the Lord forever. Therefore encourage each other with these words.*

◆ ◆ ◆

The Gifts of Hope

The gifts we've received are precious. The gift of the Holy Spirit guides us as we learn to live as God's chosen ones knowing we have the gift of an inheritance as His children. The gift of citizenship assures us belonging in God's kingdom. In great anticipation we look forward to the gift of a crown of glory as our hope is fulfilled with the gift of Jesus' presence.

Allow yourself some time to reflect on the verses from this week of Hope. Write your thoughts and reflections. Let each gift find a place in your heart.

◆ ◆ ◆

The Gift of the Holy Spirit

Acts 1:9-11
2 Corinthians 5:5

◆ ◆ ◆

The Gift of an Inheritance

1 Peter 1:3-5
Hebrews 6:19a

The Gift of Citizenship

Phillipians 3:20-21
Romans 8:24-25

The Gift of a Crown of Glory

1 Peter 5:4

1 Peter 3:15

The Gift of Jesus' Presence

1 Thessalonians 2:19-20
1 Thessalonians 4:13-18

LOVE

A GIFT FROM GOD'S HEART

Hebrews 9:27-28

> *Just as man is destined to die once, and after that to face judgement, so Christ was sacrificed once to take away the sins of many people, and he will appear a second time, not to bear sin, but to bring salvation to those who are waiting for him.*

After everything Jesus endured on earth, he is coming back. He's coming for us. That's love. God loved us so much He sent His only son years ago to take our punishment, and that profound love, just as strong as it ever was, will send Jesus back to us. Jesus loved us enough to die a horrible death for us. In John 15:13, Jesus himself explains, "Greater love has no one than this, that he lay down his life for his friends." There is no greater love than the love Jesus and God have for us.

God's own words in Jeremiah 31:3 say, "I have loved you with an everlasting love; I have drawn you with loving-kindness." God's love is everlasting. God's love reaches out to us to draw us to him. The apostle Paul wrote about God's love in Ephesians 2:1-10. He reminds Christians God's grace has saved us because of His great and merciful love for us. Not only did God save us from our sins when we were "dead in our transgressions," but He continues to love us through the ages planning to show us the "incomparable riches of his grace" in our future. His love for us was, is, and will be forever. The prophet Isaiah tells a story of God rescuing his people when there was no one else there to do it. He describes God's loving connection to His people in Isaiah 63:9 painting this picture, "In all their distress he too was distressed, and the angel of his presence saved them. In his love and mercy he redeemed them; he lifted them up and carried them all the days of old." God feels what His people feel. Love does that; love is a connection. God loves us. We are connected to God through his love. God knows every one of our successes and failures and loves us through it all. Out of that immeasurable love, God did the unthinkable and sent His own son to save us. Love came to us as one of us. And he is coming back.

When Jesus appears a second time, God will send him with a gift. A gift only God can give. A gift not of material value, but from God's own heart. A gift that will assure our presence in God's presence, because God loves us. God will send Jesus to bring us the gift of salvation.

Salvation is deliverance from harm, ruin or loss. Isaiah 51:6 describes for us a time when heaven will vanish and earth wear out and people on earth will "die like flies." But, he goes on in that verse to say salvation is forever. And Jonah proclaims in Jonah 2:9, "Salvation comes from the Lord." God gives us that forever with Him. God's salvation delivers us from sin and the consequences of sin. The consequences of our sin will harm us, ruin us and cause us to be lost from God's kingdom. We have no other deliverance from our sin besides Jesus's sacrifice of love. When Peter and John were brought before the Sanhedrin and questioned after they healed a crippled man, Peter credited Jesus with the miracle stating clearly in Acts 4:12, "Salvation is found in no one else, for there is no other name under heaven given to men by which we must be saved."

During the second week of Advent we consider love. We sometimes struggle to uncover the depth of a word so overused in our world, but the Bible tells us simply and directly - God is love. God and everything He does for us is love. God feeling our distress. God sending a savior. God rescuing us. God planning a future with us. God offering us salvation to wipe out the sin in our lives so we can live with Him in his heaven forever and ever is love. Jesus will bring us that gift of salvation on the last day offering us a lifetime in heaven saturated in God's love.

2 Thessalonians 3:5

May the Lord direct your hearts into God's love and Christ's perseverance.

THE GIFT OF A LIFETIME

Jude 1:21

> *Keep yourselves in God's love as you wait for the mercy of our Lord Jesus Christ to bring you to eternal life.*

We wait. In his mercy, Jesus will come. Jesus will bring us to eternal life. While we wait, we strive to remain enveloped in God's love. It is God's love and our faith in His love that will sustain us until we are with Him in heaven.

Jude directs us to "keep" ourselves in God's love. Action is required. Our action. God's love is abundant and available, but it is up to us to stay immersed in it. "Scoffers," Jude tells us, will be among us following their own desires apart from God. These people will divide the Christians. His warning comes directly from the apostles. It's not a new warning; it is continual. Jude encourages Christians together to build themselves up in faith in Jude 1:20. In 1 Thessalonians 5:11, Paul wrote, "Therefore encourage one another and build each other up, just as in fact you are doing." Jude also directs us to pray in the Holy Spirit. Luke tells the story in Luke 22:40 of the disciples falling asleep in the garden while Jesus prayed. Jesus told them to pray that they not fall into temptation. Even the disciples, in Jesus's presence, were threatened by temptation. Prayer through His Holy Spirit is the barrier of love God gives us against temptations. His love is stronger. As we keep ourselves in God's love, His love for us will keep us safe while we are waiting.

As we wait together, God's love doesn't end with us, it flows through us. Keeping ourselves in God's love overflows into the lives around us. Jude and Paul both give us direction to share that overflow of love helping others remain in God's love. In Jude 1:22-23, he directs us with these words, "Be merciful to those who doubt; snatch others from the fire and save them; to others show mercy, mixed with fear – hating even the clothing stained by corrupted flesh." In love, we must save each other. Paul writes in 1 Thessalonians 5:14-15, "And we urge you, brothers, warn those who are idle, encourage the timid, help the weak, be patient with everyone. Make sure that nobody pays back wrong for wrong, but always try to be kind to each other and to everyone else." God's love in us reaches "to each other and to everyone else." God's love doesn't end with us. God's love doesn't end. It is eternal.

Eternal life is God's plan for us. Eternal life in His love. Keeping ourselves in God's love sustains us on earth while we wait for Jesus to come a second time, offer us salvation and give us the gift of eternal life. A life in heaven immersed in God's love without the temptations, troubles and heartaches of our earthly lives is the gift he holds as we wait.

God chose eternity for us so long ago. Ecclesiastes 3:11 tells us, "He has made everything beautiful in its time. He has also set eternity in the hearts of men; yet they cannot fathom what God has done from beginning to end." Jesus knew. As his time to die drew near, Jesus prayed acknowledging his authority from God to give eternal life to his people saying in John 17:3, "Now this is eternal life; that they may know you, the only true God, and Jesus Christ, whom you have sent." Jesus knew he was sent to us to open the door to eternal life. Jesus showed us, with his own life, how to keep ourselves in God's love. He showed mercy and patience. He encouraged the timid. He helped the weak. He warned against idle behavior. 1 John 5:11-12 testifies, "...God has given us eternal life, and this life is in his Son. He who has the Son has life, he who does not have the Son of God does not have life."

Eternal life is a precious gift held in God's hands for each of us. He offers His love to protect us, His Son to show us and His Holy Spirit to guide us. We wait, with faith in God's love, until it is time for Jesus to take us to receive His gift.

Romans 6:23

> *For the wages of sin is death, but the gift of God is eternal life in Christ Jesus our Lord.*

A WRITTEN GIFT

2 Timothy 4:1-2

> *In the presence of God and of Christ Jesus, who will judge the living and the dead, and in view of his appearing and his kingdom, I give you this charge: Preach the Word; be prepared in season and out of season, correct, rebuke and encourage – with great patience and careful instruction.*

Timothy didn't have the New Testament. He was living it. Timothy was being taught and mentored by those who witnessed Christ's life and the lives of his disciples. In this letter, Paul knows his time on earth is close to an end, and he wants to be sure Timothy is clear how to carry on the work of making disciples for Jesus. First, he reminds him God and Jesus are present with him, and Jesus, our judge, will be appearing again establishing his kingdom. Then comes the charge. Speak God's truths, instructions, compassions and love. Always be prepared for Jesus to come again. Shepherd God's flock patiently correcting them, sternly disapproving of wrongful behavior and carefully encouraging them to continue in God's ways. Everything Timothy had learned, he now would teach. The charge is the same for all Christians. It's the same for us.

God loves all of us so deeply he sends those of us who have already received His love to share it with those who haven't. Unlike Timothy, we don't get a letter written specifically to us to tell us how to share God's tremendous love. We get them all. God didn't just give us His love, He wrote it down for us. To guide us, to remind us, to rebuke us, to encourage us, to comfort us, God gave us His words in our Bibles. God has given us the gift of His Word.

This gift is one to be unwrapped again and again and again. Every time we open scripture and read from His word, we receive His gift again. His gift is perfect. 2 Samuel 22:31a tells us, "As for God, his way is perfect; the word of the Lord is flawless." His gift gives us clear direction. "Your word is a lamp to my feet and a light for my path." (Psalm 119:105) His gift protects us. "Take the helmet of salvation and the sword of the Spirit, which is the word of God." (Ephesians 6:17) His gift guides us as we share it with others. "Let the word of Christ dwell in you richly as you teach and admonish one another with all wisdom, and as you sing psalms, hymns and spiritual songs with gratitude in your heart." (Colossians 3:16) His gift will never end. "Heaven and earth will pass away, but my words will never pass away." (Matthew 24:35)

In His love for us, God not only provides a way for each of us to be with Him forever with His gifts of salvation and eternal life, He left us a gift in our present time to remind us of His love, instruct us in His wisdom and guide us in our lives. It's a gift we can read every day. It's a gift of His love held in our hands and written on our hearts. And He asks us to share it in our actions and our words in our everyday lives. When we share the love God has given us, we show our love to Him. When we respond with God's love to others, we open a window for them to see God. When we are faithful to God's love in our actions and our speech, we allow Him to reach others through us. The love He gives us should be a refreshing fountain, not a deep, dark well. And the word of God is an everflowing stream of love that supplies our fountains.

This second week of Advent we focus on God's love for us. It isn't only evident in His promises for eternity or the blessings He has already given us. It's also evident in the way He cares for us, guides us, protects us and comforts us. His word written in our Bibles holds His truths, His compassions, His instructions and His love for us in a way we can read it and understand it for ourselves with the help of the Holy Spirit He has left with us. Until Jesus comes again for us, this gift is our treasure.

Jeremiah 23:28a

> *Let the prophet who has a dream tell his dream, but let the one who has my word speak it faithfully.*

THE GIFT ANOTHER BRINGS

Hebrews 10:25

> *Let us not give up meeting together, as some are in the habit of doing, but let us encourage one another – and all the more as you see the Day approaching.*

Fellowship. Friendship. Community. This gift has always been God's plan. God sent us each other so we can meet together, build each other up and encourage each other while we accomplish His purposes on earth waiting for Jesus's return. The gift of fellowship.

Eve brought the first gift of fellowship. God sent her to Adam so he would not be alone. God said Himself in

Genesis 2:18, "It is not good for the man to be alone. I will make a helper suitable for him." Later in Genesis is Noah's story. God instructed him to take his wife, his sons and their wives with him in the ark. Aaron was chosen by God to go with Moses as he led God's people out of Egypt. Lot accompanied Abram who later rescued Lot. David had many in his support and a true friend in Jonathan. In the New Testament, Mary and Elizabeth were gifts of support and encouragement to each other as they rejoiced in the babies they carried. Paul took great comfort in his friendship with Timothy and many others he names in his letters. Jesus was not alone, either, surrounded by his disciples.

God has given us each other and intends for us to share life together. 1 John 1:5-7 says, "This is the message we have heard from him and declare to you: God is light; in him there is no darkness at all. If we claim to have fellowship with him yet walk in the darkness, we lie and do not live by the truth. But if we walk in the light, as he is in the light, we have fellowship with one another, and the blood of Jesus, his Son, purifies us from all sin." As we remain in God's love and keep ourselves in His light, we have fellowship. Jesus said in Matthew 18:19-20, "Again, I tell you that if two of you on earth agree about anything you ask for, it will be done for you by my Father in heaven. For where two or three come together in my name, there am I with them." This fellowship is not only with each other; it includes Jesus when we are together in his name. The gift of fellowship to us includes Jesus.

It includes every one of us and is both given and received by every one of us. The gift of fellowship is a double gift. In our friendships and in our faith communities, the gift of fellowship is reciprocal. Meeting with a friend, sharing our lives, praying together and studying our Bibles, we have not only invited Jesus to be with us, but we have shared God's gift with each other. We've given encouragement and support. We've received encouragement and support. Receiving this gift of God's love through others is just as vital to us as sharing His love with others. In Bible studies, in Sunday school time, praising together in church services, in women's ministries, men's ministries, vacation bible school planning meetings, small group coffee time, or tea with a friend, we are offering God's gift and receiving it in our own lives.

In this second week of Advent we consider God's love. We know of His love for us. We know we will live in His love in heaven. We know He sent Jesus out of His love for us. Do we see His love given to us through our fellowship circles? Have we recognized their support as God's love? God reaches out to us in so many ways throughout our lives, and we miss much of it. God chose fellowship for us right here on earth. He sent other Christian people into our lives and asks us to spend time with them, encourage them, accept them, share His love with them and accept His love from them, too. And, there in the middle of it all, Jesus is included. When he comes again, we will experience the full glory of His love, and here, on earth, we can experience a glimpse of it through others in His gift of fellowship.

Romans 15:5-7

> *May the God who gives endurance and encouragement give you a spirit of unity among yourselves as you follow Christ Jesus so that with one heart and mouth you may glorify the God and Father of our Lord Jesus Christ.*

A MERCIFUL GIFT

2 Peter 3:8-9

> *But do not forget this one thing, dear friends: With the Lord a day is like a thousand years, and a thousand years is like a day. The Lord is not slow in keeping his promise, as some understand slowness. He is patient with you, not wanting anyone to perish, but everyone to come to repentance.*

God isn't bound by our calendar. Peter explained in his letter because so many were expecting Jesus to return soon, in their lifetime, and they were feeling discouraged. God will keep His promise to send Jesus back for us, but He is patiently waiting for His children to repent, live their lives in His love and share that love with others so they, too, will not perish.

God has been patient for a very long time. In Nehemiah 9, the story is told of the Israelites journey from Egypt with all the miracles God performed while He led them to the promised land, yet they did not obey the commands. Verse 17 says, "But you are a forgiving God, gracious and compassionate, slow to anger and abounding in love. Therefore, you did not desert them..." In God's compassion He waited for His people to come back to Him offering forgiveness when they repented. The prophet Jeremiah was offered that same patience and forgiveness when he became frustrated waiting for God to act. In Jeremiah 15:19, God replied to his complaining saying, "If you repent, I will restore you that you may serve me." God didn't give up on Jeremiah.

God doesn't give up on us. Romans 3:23 assures us, "for all have sinned and fall short of the glory of God." However, Peter reminds us in 2 Peter 3:15, "Bear in mind that our Lord's patience means salvation, just as our dear brother Paul also wrote you with the wisdom that God gave him." Like Jeremiah, God wants to restore us so we can serve Him now and receive His salvation forever.

Paul spoke often of repentance reminding Christians they should "prove their repentance by their deeds." Luke, too, used words from John the Baptist instructing the people, "Produce fruit in keeping with repentance." God is waiting for that fruit in our lives. While we learn to live in His love, He gives to us His gift of patience.

Psalm 130 passionately describes our dependence on the Lord, our need for His forgiveness and the promises we have in Him. His love is "unfailing" and we can expect "full redemption." As we wait for the Lord and put our hope in His promises, we make mistakes, repent, learn His ways and begin to produce fruit. He patiently teaches us through His word, through other Christians, and through our life situations. As we learn, He is patient. When we grow impatient He asks us to repent again, learn again and produce more fruit. Eventually our lives will be more fruitful than not when we follow His instructions and learn to live through His unfailing love. We fail. God does not. His gift of patience carries us during those times.

Trusting in His patience and learning to live in His love, we begin to bear fruit. Proverbs 11:30 tells us, “The fruit of the righteous is a tree of life, and he who wins souls is wise.” God does not want anyone to perish and wants everyone to come to repentance. Our fruit draws others to God. His gift of patience affords us wisdom. Matthew 7:15-16 warns us of false prophets coming in sheep’s clothing, yet, “by their fruit you will recognize them.” As we become more fruitful, gaining in wisdom, we are more able to discern the false prophets by their fruit and avoid their deception. Continuing in God’s love we aspire to live by the Spirit and bear the fruit of the Spirit – love, joy, peace, patience, kindness, goodness, faithfulness, gentleness and self-control. (Galatians 5:22-23a) God waits patiently.

The gift of God’s patience in our lives binds us in His love while we learn to live fruitfully for Him waiting for Jesus to return for us.

2 Peter 3:18

> *But grow in grace and knowledge of our Lord and Savior Jesus Christ. To him be glory both now and forever! Amen.*

◆ ◆ ◆

The Gifts of Love

There is no greater love anywhere, ever, than God's love for us. His love is present and here with us now in His written word and in the fellowship of His believers. God's word and Jesus's life instruct us and guide us as we keep ourselves in His love. He patiently guides and waits as we learn His ways and share His love with others. His plan for us is salvation and eternal life.

Immerse yourself in God's love as you reflect on the verses from this week of Love. Write your thoughts, prayers and praises. Open a place in your heart for each of these gifts.

◆ ◆ ◆

A Gift from God's Heart

Hebrews 9:27-28
2 Thessalonians 3:5

◆ ◆ ◆

The Gift of a Lifetime

Jude 1:21
Romans 6:23

◆ ◆ ◆

A Written Gift

2 Timothy 4:1-2
Jeremiah 23:28a

◆ ◆ ◆

The Gift Another Brings

Hebrews 10:25
Romans 15:5-7

◆ ◆ ◆

A Merciful Gift

2 Peter 3:8-9
2 Peter 3:18

JOY

AN ANTICIPATED GIFT

Micah 5:2

> *"But you, Bethlehem Ephrathah, though you are small among the clans of Judah, out of you will come for me one who will be ruler over Israel, whose origins are from old, from ancient times."*

Destruction. Judgement. Chaos. Fear. Those were the messages the prophet Micah brought to the Israelites. They were under siege. But then, for those who believed, he had more. God had plans. A ruler for Israel out of one of the small clans. A ruler who would come from eternity. Amid warnings about the destruction to come with God's judgement, Micah lit the flame of hope and anticipation for those who truly believed.

We know that hope. We marvel in the hope of Jesus coming back just as the Israelites marveled in the hope of a coming savior. We anticipate a life with our Heavenly King just as the Israelites anticipated a life with their promised ruler. Those who believed learned to trust God's plan as they anticipated the arrival of the ruler from Bethlehem to make their joy complete. Their joy was found in a baby. A baby whose birth marked the beginning of a new time. Our joy is found in that manger, too. Jesus, from his birth to our lives now and forever is the source of our joy. God sent Jesus to live among us to captivate our hearts and turn to Him. Joy in a relationship with God through His son, Jesus Christ. That immense joy came wrapped up in one little baby. Micah tells us God planned that little baby ages before his birth. God's plans for us all included Jesus from the very beginning, ancient times, eternity.

Exquisitely offered in Jesus's birth, God planned the joy Jesus brought. Abram was not a remarkable man, yet God promised him in Genesis 12:3, "I will bless those who bless you, and whoever curses you I will curse; and all peoples on earth will be blessed through you." That promise of a blessing for all peoples continued through Abram's lineage right up to an ordinary shepherd boy, David. 2 Samuel 7:16 records God's promise to David, "Your house and your kingdom will endure forever before me, your throne will be established forever." Baby Jesus was the deliverance of that promise.

We live within that delivered promise. "All peoples

on earth will be blessed through you." We are those people. Joy! Our joy does not depend on the future, we have hope for that. Our joy is right now. Jesus brought joy into the world when he brought God's love in human form. The joy of his presence in our world remains with us. God had plans including us from the very beginning. Those plans of joy in our lives are one of His best gifts to us. When God sent Jesus as a tiny baby into our world, He was planning for us. He offered us joy for our lives right now just because we know Jesus.

As we celebrate the birth of Jesus during this third week of Advent, we imagine the joy the Israelites who believed must've felt at the long-awaited arrival of the Christ Child. Luke tells the stories in Luke 2:25-32 of Simeon and in verses 36-38 of the prophetess Anna. Both Simeon and Anna waited for God's Christ to redeem Jerusalem and were overjoyed to see baby Jesus in the temple courts. Shepherds left their flocks to witness the baby, and wise men traveled for months. They felt the joy of God's promise in the baby and excitement of a future in God's plans.

God's plans include us. The joy of Jesus birth is for us, too. All of us. Bethlehem was only a small town. Simeon only one man. Anna a widow. Abram and his wife, Sarai, were childless nomads from a pagan family. David was a shepherd boy. Joseph was only a carpenter and Mary a young girl pledged in marriage. None noteworthy, yet all significant. God includes us all in the glorious promise and birth of Jesus. Like the times of

Micah, we may be under siege. There may be chaos and destruction around us, but we already have the joy of Jesus's birth and his exquisite presence in our lives.

The candle of joy we light in our Advent wreaths this week intensifies the flames of hope and love. Strengthened by the joy in the birth of our Lord, we have hope and witness His love. Three flames shining brightly to guide us in God's plans.

Matthew 1:18

> *This is how the birth of Jesus Christ came about: His mother Mary was pledged to be married to Joseph, but before they came together, she was found to be with child through the Holy Spirit.*

A HUMBLE GIFT

Isaiah 7:14

> *Therefore the Lord himself will give you a sign: The virgin will be with child and will give birth to a son, and will call him Immanuel.*

It was another parting of the waters. In their fear of angering God, testing His limits, God's people wouldn't ask for a sign that He was with them. Ahaz was leading his people to fight against Jerusalem but he lost his resolve. He was afraid of the enemy. God sent the prophet, Isaiah, to encourage Ahaz to stand firm in his faith. The warriors were drowning in an ocean of fear. Then God offered a sign, without a request, parting the waters of their fear and promising them a son called "God with us." His assurance beckoned them to continue in their battle and trust God had their future in control. They wanted to be assured of

God's spiritual presence. They received, also, a promise of his physical presence to come.

The Israelites knew God was mighty. Moses's stories of God's might went all the way back to Egypt recorded in Exodus 6:1, "Then the Lord said to Moses, "Now you will see what I will do to Pharoah: Because of my mighty hand he will let them go; because of my mighty hand he will drive them out of his country." They knew to rely on His strength and might and to pray for His presence with them in their battles. Psalm 50:1 describes God as a "Mighty One" who directs even the rising and setting of the sun. Psalm 24:8 asks, "Who is this King of glory? The Lord strong and mighty, the Lord mighty in battle." They relied on God's presence to encourage them, strengthen them, fortify them, guide them and save them. At every turn God knew what His people needed. Psalm 147:5 tells us, "Great is our Lord and mighty in power, his understanding has no limits." God led them out of Egypt with a cloud and fire, He fed them in the desert, He struck down their enemies and gave them the "land of milk and honey," He guided them in the battle of Jericho, His strength had no end.

Yet, He came as a baby. All the strength and might of God embodied in a tiny, helpless, humble baby. Jesus brought God to be with us in a human form we could understand and emulate. A person we could touch and see and believe. God humbled himself to gain our devotion. He lovingly and gently reached down from heaven and placed Jesus among us, capturing our attention and drawing us near. God gave us the gift of His own presence in Jesus.

The joy of God with us was celebrated even before the virgin birth. When Mary went to visit Elizabeth at the time they both were expecting their babies, Elizabeth exclaimed, "As soon as the sound of your greeting reached my ears, the baby in my womb leaped for joy." (Luke 1:44) At his birth, the angels spoke to the shepherds heralding they had "good news of great joy." The joy was no longer anticipated, He was here.

The joy of God's presence with us in His son Jesus is still here. Jesus brought us that joy, and, even though Jesus has physically left this earth, his presence in our lives remains. His joy cannot be taken from us. We have a mighty God who loves us so much He wrapped His infallible character, His flawless integrity and His unfailing love in flesh and sent it to earth to us so we could learn to live like Him. Joy that He values us worthy to be with him. Joy that He cares enough to be among us. Joy that He understood we needed Jesus. Joy that He sent him.

The joy of the Lord sent to us that night in Bethlehem is ours every day. The third Advent candle flickers at Christmas reminding us of that miraculous birth and the great gift of God's presence with us, Immanuel.

Luke 2:6-7

While they were there, the time came for the baby to be born, and she gave birth to her firstborn, a son. She wrapped him in cloths and placed him in a manger, because there was no room for them in the inn.

THE GIFT OF SPLENDOR

John 1:14

> *The Word became flesh and made his dwelling among us. We have seen his glory, the glory of the One and Only, who came from the Father, full of grace and truth.*

God's magnificence, His glory, came to earth in Baby Jesus. Hebrews 1:3a describes the eminence of Jesus's relationship with God saying, "The Son is the radiance of God's glory and the exact representation of his being, sustaining all things by his powerful word." The radiance of God's glory among His people on earth is a gift brought to us at Jesus's birth. God has given us the gift of His glory in our lives.

Moses asked to see God's glory in Exodus 33:18 when God was asking him to lead His people out of Egypt. It was Moses's final proof that it was God asking him to go to Egypt, and it was his reassurance that God would go with him. Ezekiel witnessed the glory of God in a vision he recounts in Ezekiel 43:1-5. He describes God's glory as radiant and filling the temple with God's presence and power. David describes a time in Psalms 63:2 when he saw God's glory and power in the sanctuary. Experienced by a few, God's glory was a physical manifestation of His presence and power. David paints a beautiful picture of the power of the glory of God in Psalm 19:1-4, saying, "The heavens declare the glory of God; the skies proclaim the work of his hands. Day after day they pour forth speech; night after night they display knowledge. There is no speech or language where their voice is not heard. Their voice goes out into all the earth, their words to the ends of the world." And then, in Psalm 72:19, Solomon wisely prays, "Praise be to his glorious name forever; may the whole earth be filled with his glory."

Years later, in the dark of the night, out in the fields, shepherds were watching their flocks when the glory of the Lord shone around them. (Luke 2:9) Joy! God's glory ushered in God's glory. Jesus was born. The radiance of God's glory was given to us in a tiny baby, right here on earth.

The glory of God in Jesus radiates a light for us to heaven. In Revelations 21, the new Jerusalem is being described and in verse 23, it says, “The city does not need the sun or the moon to shine on it, for the glory of God gives it light, and the Lamb is its lamp.” Jesus radiated God’s glory from the beginning. In John 17, Jesus is praying for himself before his arrest. Knowing his time had come, Jesus prays to be glorified so He can glorify God. He describes eternal life as knowing God and Jesus Christ. He acknowledges he has completed the work God gave him on earth bringing glory to God, then he asks, “And now, Father, glorify me in your presence with the glory I had with you before the world began.” Jesus was the radiance of God’s glory before he became man. He brought that glory to earth to shine a light for all of us to follow him to heaven to live forever in God’s glory there. Joy!

We only need to look to Jesus to experience God’s glory. The life Jesus led, the parables he spoke, the truths he shared are all part of that glory. Everything Jesus did, everything Jesus said are within that beacon of light that redirects our paths towards God and a life with Him in heaven. Having lived on earth as a human with us, Jesus’s life light cannot be snuffed out now. We have the stories, we have the scriptures, we have his words and his actions therefore, we have his glory available to us at any moment when we choose to focus on his brilliance.

The presence of God’s glory brings us joy. Our joy in His presence continues to radiate His light to others around us. The third Advent candle is a tiny beacon of that light reminding us of the more glorious light He offers for those who seek. Joy in God's glory.

2 Corinthians 3:18

> *And we, who with unveiled faces all reflect the Lord's glory, are being transformed into his likeness with ever-increasing glory, which comes from the Lord, who is the Spirit.*

A SHARED GIFT

Luke 2:10

> *But the angel said to them, "Do not be afraid. I bring you good news of great joy that will be for all the people."*

In the night darkness when the glory of the Lord suddenly shone around them, the shepherds were terrified. A heralding, brilliant angel spoke, dissolving their fears into excitement with the promise of great joy. They must've been shocked and certainly curious. Shepherds were quite often despised and considered unclean and untrustworthy by the orthodox Jewish people. An angel appearing to them was quite unexpected. They may have known the expectations of a new ruler for the Jewish people. They most likely had heard the stories and prophecies. They may have even understood the excitement of the most religious people and acknowledged their excitement would be realized one day, but did they consider that excitement for themselves, too? Working continually to feed their flocks and care for them in rugged conditions, in tents without the comforts of a home, did the shepherds even have time to think about how it would all happen? They lived on the fringes, and they knew it.

In that magnificent, glory filled moment in the presence of God's angels, those same shepherds, deemed unworthy, heard these words, "great joy that will be for all the people." All. In their soiled, sheep smelling clothes and unkempt faces, they were included. Joy was for them, too.

God's joy, swaddled in an innocent newborn, extended to His people, all His people, is for us, too. We are included. God has given us the gift of inclusion. His joy is not only for the Jewish people, but for all of us who will accept Him, no matter who we are, what we have done, how much we have, or how we were raised. Luke 19 tells the story of Zacchaeus the tax collector. The people considered him a "sinner" and didn't appreciate Jesus spending time with him, but Zacchaeus recognized Jesus and repented. In verses 9-10 Jesus says to him, "Today salvation has come to this house, because this man, too, is a son of Abraham. For the Son of Man came to seek and to save what was lost." Zacchaeus, a sinner, accepted God's joy. In Romans 10:20, the Apostle Paul defends the truth that Jesus is a savior also to Gentiles and recounts Isaiah's words of prophecy, "I was found by those who did not seek me. I revealed myself to those who did not ask for me." (Isaiah 42:6) More clearly, the Apostle Paul writes in Romans 1:16, "I am not ashamed of the gospel, because it is the power of God for the salvation of everyone who believes: first for the Jew, then for the Gentile." In Romans 10:12, he proclaims, "For there is no difference between Jew and Gentile – the same Lord is Lord of all and richly blesses all who call on him, for, "Everyone who calls on the name of the Lord will be saved." (Joel 2:32)

Joy for us all. John 16:24 tells us, "Until now you have not asked for anything in my name. Ask and you will receive, and your joy will be complete." Jesus was born to include all of us in God's joy. He was given to us. He gives us God's joy. We only need to ask in Jesus's name.

Renewing our joy in Jesus during Advent asks us to re-focus on Jesus. It asks us to blur the judgements we impose on others so we instead can see Jesus in every-one who believes and rejoice together with all people who have accepted God's joy in Jesus. Those in our families, those in our workplace, those in our churches and those on the fringes all celebrate the joy of Jesus. Like the strength of the Advent candle's flames burning together, we can shine the light of Jesus brighter and reach more of the lost in his name when we join our flames in unity in the joy of Jesus this Christmas.

John 1:12-13

Yet to all who received him, to those who believed

in his name he gave the right to become children of God – children born not of natural descent, nor of human decision or a husband's will, but born of God.

A PROMISED GIFT FULFILLED

Isaiah 61:1-3

> *The Spirit of the Sovereign Lord is on me, because the Lord has anointed me to preach good news to the poor. He has sent me to bind up the broken hearted, to proclaim freedom for the captives and release from darkness for the prisoners, to proclaim the year of the Lord's favor and the day of vengeance of our God, to comfort all who mourn and provide for those who grieve in Zion – to bestow on them a crown of beauty instead of ashes, the oil of gladness instead of mourning, and a garment of praise instead of a spirit of despair. They will be called oaks of righteousness, a planting of the Lord for the day of his splendor.*

Luke 4:16-21

He went to Nazareth, where he had been brought up, and on the sabbath day he went into the synagogue, as was his custom. And he stood up to read. The scroll of the prophet Isaiah was handed to him. Unrolling it he found the place where it is written: "The Spirit of the Lord is on me because he has anointed me to preach good news to the poor. He has sent me to proclaim freedom to the prisoners and recovery of sight to the blind, to release the oppressed, to proclaim the year of the Lord's favor. Then he rolled up the scroll, gave it back to the attendant and sat down. The eyes of everyone in the synagogue were fastened on him, and he began by saying to them, "Today this scripture is fulfilled in your hearing."

Jesus was home, in Nazareth. He went to the synagogue just like every other sabbath day he spent at home. He must've informed the one in charge of the synagogue service he wished to speak, as was the custom for men. When he stood to read scripture for the service, he didn't choose which scroll to read, yet Isaiah's was handed to him. At the end of the reading, Jesus sat down to distinguish his commentary from the scripture he was reading as was also the synagogue custom. Usually the speaker linked the reading with other texts. All eyes were on him. And he said, "Today this scripture is fulfilled in your hearing." Unexpected. As he continued to speak he proclaimed he would not be accepted in his hometown just as prophets were not accepted in theirs, and the people became furious and drove him away. They missed the joy.

Don't miss the joy! God's gift of scriptures fulfilled is saturated with promise and joy. During this Advent week we focus on the baby Jesus and all the scriptures his presence with us fulfills. This scripture from Isaiah brims with hope for everyone.

Jesus came to preach good news to the poor. Matthew 5:3 says, "Blessed are the poor in spirit, for theirs is the kingdom of heaven." Poor isn't only our economical situation. 2 Corinthians 8:9 tells us, "For you know the grace of our Lord Jesus Christ, that though he was rich, yet for your sakes he became poor, so that you through his poverty might become rich." Jesus set aside the riches of his heavenly existence to take on flesh and lead us home to heaven. Whether we are poor in living conditions, in spirit or in knowledge, Jesus came to show us God's heaven offers us more, and he shows us the way to heaven. Joy.

Jesus came to proclaim freedom to the prisoners. Galatians 3:22 reminds us, "But the Scripture declares that the whole world is a prisoner of sin, so that what was promised, being given through faith in Jesus Christ, might be given to those who believe." We are all prisoners. Jesus offers us freedom. Joy.

Jesus came to release the oppressed. Psalm 9:9 reminds us God's people already knew God sheltered the oppressed, "The Lord is a refuge for the oppressed, a stronghold in times of trouble." Zechariah 10:2 illuminates the cause of oppression, "The idols speak deceit, diviners see visions that lie, they tell dreams that are false, they give comfort in vain. Therefore the people wander like sheep oppressed for lack of a shepherd." Jesus is our shepherd. Jesus was born to us to release us from oppression as he shepherds us to heaven. Joy.

God's joy is ours once we accept His gifts. Jesus was born to show us the way. He brought God's joy down to us from heaven and guides us to live in that joy everyday as we learn to rely on God. Like the people in Nazareth, we will miss the joy if we don't place our faith in Jesus and allow him to give us good news, proclaim our freedom and release our oppression. He came to do those things for us. Joy.

John 3:4-6

> *As is written in the words of the book of Isaiah the prophet: "A voice of one calling in the desert, 'Prepare the way for the Lord, make straight paths for him. Every valley shall be filled in, every moun-*

tain and hill made low. The crooked roads shall become straight, the rough ways smooth. And all mankind will see God's salvation."

The Gifts of Joy

Humbly, God brought Jesus to us so we could experience His joy in our lives. Jesus, the radiance of God's glory, illuminates the way to life eternal with God, a life offered to everyone who accepts the Son. Fulfilling the scriptures, the Sonship of Jesus cannot be denied and proves the source of significant joy for believers. Joy is ours today, tomorrow and forever in the birth of Jesus Christ.

Take some time to put yourself in the Christmas story. Imagine the great joy believers felt. Consider what life would be like without the light of Jesus on our paths. Claim the joy he offers right now. Write your thoughts as you reflect on the verses this week.

An Anticipated Gift

Micah 5:2
Matthew 1:18

◆ ◆ ◆

A Humble Gift

Isaiah 7:14
Luke 2:6-7

◆ ◆ ◆

The Gift of Splendor

John 1:14
2 Corinthians 3:18

A Shared Gift

Luke 2:10
John 1:12-13

A Promised Gift Fulfilled

Isaiah 61:1-3
Luke 4:16-21
John 3:4-6

PEACE

A COMPASSIONATE GIFT

Luke 2:14

> *"Glory to God in the Highest, and on earth peace to men on whom his favor rests."*

Imagine the spectacular harmony of a "great company of heavenly host" joining God's angel in praise. The shepherds experienced it. The praises were heard in the very heaven of heavens, the Highest. Something incredible was happening, and God was being praised. Enrapt in glorious admiration, the focus shifts. Peace to men on earth who please God.

The New International Version translation says, "to

men on whom his favor rests." The English Standard Version says, "among those with whom he is pleased." The Message Bible expounds on the verse, "to all men and women on earth who please him." And, the King James Version translates the passage, "goodwill toward men." God's good will toward men brought Jesus Christ to us for the redemption of the world. That redemption is designed for God's glory. He wants us. He wants us to trust Him, obey Him and be present with Him forever. He chose to send Jesus to us to guide us to Him, to show us how to please Him, and to exemplify the peace we can have when we walk in His ways. Isaiah foretells of Jesus coming in Isaiah 9:6 describing, "For to us a child is born, to us a son is given, and the government will be on his shoulders. And he will be called Wonderful Counselor, Mighty God, Everlasting Father, Prince of Peace. Zechariah describes Jesus's rule, and, in Zechariah 9:10, tells us, "He will proclaim peace to the nations." God's gift of good will toward us brought us Jesus and brings us peace as we live on earth. Peace for those who please God.

David understood. In Psalm 34:14 he directs us, "Turn from evil and do good; seek peace and pursue it." Turn. Seek. Pursue. Claiming peace requires our action. When we turn from evil thoughts and actions, we turn toward God's peace. When we seek peace, we find Jesus's examples. When we pursue peace, we walk in the light of Jesus on the path to God and His plans for our lives. And our faith strengthens. Peter mirrored David's thoughts in 1 Peter 3:10-11 writing, "For, Whoever would love life and see good days must keep their tongue from evil and their lips from deceitful speech. They must turn from evil and do good; they must seek peace and pursue it." Believers in David's day relied on the stories and examples from Godly followers before them. Believers in Peter's day and in ours have the life of Jesus and his words and examples to follow. God infused our world with His peace when He sent His son.

It's comforting to think of the peace of heaven in our future. It's easy to miss the peace of God we can experience right now. We are God's people, and His peace is available to us. Ephesians 2:14-16 says, "For he himself is our peace, who has made the two groups one and has destroyed the barrier, the dividing wall of hostility, by setting aside in his flesh the law with its command and regulations. His purpose was to create in himself one new humanity out of the two, thus making peace, and in one body to reconcile both of them to God through the cross, by which he put to death their hostility." Jesus's birth brought all believers together in peace. In peace we can work together to accomplish His purposes.

The fourth week of Advent reminds us of the peace we find in Jesus's birth and his life. In all the world's turmoil, in the busiest week before Christmas, we must take time to turn, seek and pursue the peace Jesus brought to us in that lowly manger. The true message of Christmas will be magnified in the examples of God's believers as the world focuses on our faith during this season. The peace we find in Jesus will shine the true

Christmas lights through our lives for the world to follow. God's gift of good will lights a flame in each believer illuminating His peace in the world.

Romans 5:1

> *Therefore, since we have been justified through faith, we have peace with God through our Lord Jesus Christ.*

A CALMING GIFT

Zechariah 9:9-10

Rejoice greatly, O Daughter of Zion! Shout, Daughter of Jerusalem! See, your king comes to you righteous and having salvation, gentle and riding on a donkey, on a colt, the foal of a donkey. I will take away the chariots from Ephraim and the war-horses from Jerusalem, and the battle bow will be broken. He will proclaim peace to the nations. His rule will extend from sea to sea and from the river to the ends of the earth.

John 12:14-15

Jesus found a young donkey and sat upon it, as it is written, "Do not be afraid, O Daughter of Zion, see, your king is coming, seated on a donkey's colt."

Prophecy fulfilled! Old Testament believers had prophecies and were encouraged and strengthened by them. They waited in great anticipation, believing in a God they never saw but in His strength they experienced. Believers in Jesus's time experienced the prophecies being fulfilled and were amazed and excited. They raised the banners and followed Jesus, believing in a God they could now see and witnessing His power. Now, believers have both. We experience His strength, we witness His power and we see His example in Jesus's life. We read His prophecies and their fulfillments. God kept His promises. He still does. We have no reason to fear. Jesus calms our spirits with God's gift of replacing our fear with His peace. Jesus brought us that peace when he arrived in the stable. He is the visible, touchable, speakable peace of God in our world. His arrival has the power to take away our fear.

Jesus showed no fear. He had no fear. He was one with God, and He trusted God to take care of all his needs. He was tempted by the devil in the desert, in the Holy City and on a high mountain in Matthew 4:1-11, yet Jesus was not afraid and resisted temptation. Each time Jesus rebuked the devil with quotes from Deuteronomy magnifying his trust and understanding of God. During the Lord's Supper in the upper room, Jesus knew his time was near, yet he was not afraid. In Mark 14:25, he reveals his rightful home with God when he says, "I tell you the truth, I will not drink again of the fruit of the vine until that day when I drink it anew in the kingdom of God." When he was betrayed and arrested, he showed compassion instead of fear healing an ear sliced in anger. (Luke 22: 50-51) Then, arrested and questioned by the chief priests and teachers Jesus again asserted he would be seated at the right hand of God, knowing God's will. As he was beaten and crucified, he displayed no fear. John 19:28-30 records Jesus's last words, "Later, knowing that all was now completed, and so that the Scripture would be fulfilled, Jesus said, "I am thirsty." A jar of wine vinegar was there, so they soaked a sponge in it, put the sponge on a stalk of the hyssop plant, and lifted it to Jesus's lips. When he had received the drink, Jesus said, "It is finished." With that, he bowed his head and gave up his spirit." In his worst times, Jesus leaned on the will of God and had no fear. He displayed for us God's peace even in his hardest hour.

God's peace replaces our fear when we learn to walk with Jesus in close personal relationship with God. Jesus, God's own son, extends the peace he lived to us through his life with us and through the Holy Spirit he left in us. Romans 8:15 assures us, "For you did not receive a spirit that makes you a slave again to fear, but you received the Spirit of sonship." We've been adopted into God's family and invited through the birth of Jesus into a personal one-on-one relationship with God. As we learn His ways and rely on His word, our fears are diminished by the peace we receive.

During this last week of Advent, we are beckoned by

the flame of peace to draw near to Jesus, rely on God, claim our sonship through the Spirit and let go of our fears. God wants us to live in His peace with Him as His children.

Isaiah 43:1

> *But now, this is what the Lord says – he who created you, O Jacob, he who formed you, O Israel; "Fear not, for I have redeemed you; I have summoned you by name; you are mine.*

AN ANCHORED GIFT

Colossians 3:15

> *Let the peace of Christ rule in your hearts, since as members of one body you were called to peace. And be thankful.*

Allow the peace Jesus offers to exercise ultimate power or authority in your hearts, because as God's people that's what he asks us to do. Recognize the gift and be thankful for it. Let. Allow. It's an act of surrender not something we seize. The peace of Jesus is offered with incredible power. The peace of Jesus can rule in our hearts. The peace of Jesus can exercise ultimate power and authority in our hearts. The power of Jesus ruling our hearts in peace. And, that surrender leads us to thankfulness. What a gift!

The peace of Christ is ours. Jesus brought peace for us to witness, experience and accept when he was humbly born into our earthly world. God had given his people peace before Jesus came. God directed Moses in Numbers 6:24-26 to tell the priests to bless His people saying, “The Lord bless you and keep you, the Lord make his face shine upon you and be gracious to you; the Lord turn his face toward you and give you peace.” Yet, He recognized we still needed an anchor for our hearts, a cornerstone, a foundation to secure us and attach us to Him. He sent Jesus. Jesus is our cornerstone and our peace provider.

“Peace I leave with you; my peace I give you. I do not give to you as the world gives. Do not let your hearts be troubled and do not be afraid.” (John 14:27) Jesus has given us not just peace like we may get from our worldy pursuits, but he has given us his peace. The very peace he had when he was tempted, betrayed and beaten. That incredible peace he displayed in every circumstance in his life. The peace he felt because he was one with God and trusted God’s plans. He left that peace with us right here in our earthly world. Right here in our tangled lives. Right here for us. Anchoring our hearts to his.

Anchored to Jesus’s heart opens our eyes to see God’s work in our lives. Allowing Jesus’s peace to take control of our hearts provides Jesus’s power in our decisions and our reactions. We can overcome the negative influences in our lives. We can make better choices with the power of his peace. We can react with his love to difficult situations. We can mirror the peace Jesus demonstrated to us to those around us leading them to find Jesus's peace in their own lives. Allowing Jesus's peace to rule in our hearts allows God to use our lives to strengthen His kingdom.

Peace is God's desire for his people. Isaiah 26:3 tells us, "You will keep in perfect peace all who trust in you, all whose thoughts are fixed on you!" God lovingly placed His perfect peace in our world in a tiny infant for us to see, experience and believe. Jesus is perfect peace. When we trust in God and focus our thoughts on His ways, we can experience perfect peace because we are emulating Jesus.

Jesus, our Prince of Peace, offers us not only his peace but he lived his life as an example for us, showing us how to live our own lives. Jesus was a peacemaker. Following his example, we too become peacemakers. Jesus himself in Matthew 5:9 says, "Blessed are the peacemakers, for they will be called sons of God." As the only begotten son of God, Jesus lived in God's perfect peace. Accepting Jesus's peace in our lives gives us the same perfect peace since we are children of God.

Our hearts ruled by the peace of Christ is God's desire for us. During this last week of Advent we can slow down the barrage of the world and focus on the peace of the Christ child lying in a manger remembering his earthly life was for our eternal one. He lived his life to gain ours. His earthly life examples bring us closer to his perfect peace when we allow him to rule our hearts.

John 16:33

> *"I have told you these things, so that in me you may have peace. In this world you will have trouble. But take heart! I have overcome the world."*

AN INFINITE GIFT

Isaiah 9:6-7

> *For to us a child is born, to us a son is given, and the government will be on his shoulders. And he will be called Wonderful Counselor, Mighty God, Everlasting Father, Prince of Peace. Of the increase of his government and peace there will be no end. He will reign on David's throne and over his kingdom, establishing and upholding it with justice and righteousness from that time on and forever. The zeal of the Lord Almighty will accomplish this.*

Jesus is born for us. Jesus's government will always increase. His peace will always increase and never end. He will reign with justice forever. He will reign with righteousness forever. God's zeal will make it happen.

Zeal is a great energy or enthusiasm in pursuit of a cause. God's cause is His people. Us. God has always been zealous for His people, and God doesn't change. When God's people were surrounded by sinners and had turned away, God asked Noah to build a boat. When God found one man worthy of His devotion who would raise His children for God, He gave him sons even in old age then promised Abraham He would make him into "a great nation." When God knew His people needed to be released from the laws and humbly guided to a greater love, he sent Jesus. Jesus, whose reign will be established and upheld with justice and righteousness forever increasing in peace. Perfect justice and righteousness for God's people are gifts only Jesus can offer.

Isaiah told the world God's plan in Isaiah 42:4 when he said, "He will not falter or be discouraged till he establishes justice on earth. In his law the islands will put their hope." Isaiah 61:8 gives us God's own words, "For I, the Lord, love justice; I hate robbery and iniquity. In my faithfulness I will reward them and make an everlasting covenant with them." Psalms 9:16 assures us, "The Lord is known by his justice; the wicked are ensnared by the work of their hands." Justice belongs to God. Justice, when everything wrong is made right. In His zeal, He will establish His justice on earth. Jesus showed us justice at the well with the Samaritan woman. He showed us justice when he ate with Zacchaeus, each time he healed the blind and lame and drove out demons, and when he showed mercy to the little children. Wrongs made right. Compassion we can mirror. Peace we can share.

Psalm 89:14 sings praises to God acknowledging, "Righteousness and justice are the foundation of your throne; love and faithfulness go before you." Justice will be established righting every wrong and then righteousness, the quality of being morally right or justifiable, will prevail for eternity. There is no other way to envision that other than indescribable peace. And, love and faithfulness lead the way. Even now. It was God's love for us that brought us Jesus. 2 Corinthians 5:21 tells us, "God made him who had no sin to be sin for us, so that in him we might become the righteousness of God." The righteousness of God is only available to us through Jesus. Jesus who was born for us.

The flame of peace burns strong in our Advent candles this week. Under the shelter of God's love, we focus on our faithfulness during this Christmas season. Remembering the birth of Jesus reminds us of the great love God has for us and the peace He wants us to experience. Peacefully, in a lowly manger, Jesus came in God's love and faithfulness to His people. God's zeal for us brought God's heart down to us offering indescribable peace as He protects us with his own justice and righteousness. We offer our faithfulness as we learn to walk as Jesus taught us, love as Jesus did and do all we can to right wrongs and live righteously. God offers us His peace, forever, and the promise of an eternity spent in His justice and His righteousness. Psalms 85:10 says, "Love and faithfulness meet together; righteousness and peace kiss each other." This final week of Advent, rest in the love and faithfulness God showed us in the birth of the baby Jesus and allow His righteousness and His peace room in your life.

Matthew 6:33

> *But seek first his kingdom and his righteousness,*
> *and all these things will be given to you as well.*

A GUIDING GIFT

Titus 2:11-14

> *For the grace of God that brings salvation has appeared to all men. It teaches us to say "no" to ungodliness and worldly passions, and to live self-controlled, upright and godly lives in this present age, while we wait for the blessed hope – the glorious appearing of our great God, and savior, Jesus Christ, who gave himself for us to redeem us from all wickedness and to purify for himself a people that are his very own, eager to do what is good.*

The grace of God brought salvation. The grace of God has been revealed to us and teaches us. The grace of God embodied in Jesus purifies us. Purified, we are eager to do what is good. God's grace is the gift. Within it we find peace.

God's grace is so much more than just His unmerited favor or an unearned benefit for us. Wrapped up in God's grace is His amazing gift of forgiveness of our sins. Inside the gift he offers His power to us to live in the present with dignity and hope in the future. Isaiah tells us in Isaiah 30:18, "Yet the Lord longs to be gracious to you; he rises to show you compassion. For the Lord is a God of justice. Blessed are all who wait for him!" God longs to be gracious to us. He yearns to show us His compassion. In His desperation to reach us He gave His only son to live among us so we could experience God's grace and compassion and follow Jesus home to Him. Following Jesus, we wait for God. Remembering Jesus's examples, we trust God's timing, His choices, His justice. We wait peacefully in His power knowing He is in control. Like Jesus, we experience his graciousness in our wait. John 1:17 says, "For the law was given through Moses; grace and truth came through Jesus Christ." God sent His grace in visible, touchable, believable form because God longs for us to be with Him in His peace. The Apostle Paul wrote in Ephesians 2:6-7, "And God raised us up with Christ and seated us with him in the heavenly realms in Christ Jesus, in order that in the coming ages he might show the incomparable riches of his grace, expressed in his kindness to us in Christ Jesus."

Jesus showed us God's grace. Born into this world just like we were, Jesus experienced the life we live, the temptations we face, the sorrows we experience, the injustices we are dealt and the bonds of friendship we embrace. Trusting in God's plans, He demonstrated love, self-control, compassion, and devotion. And Jesus demonstrated it all with indescribable peace. Paul exemplifies that peace when, from prison, he wrote in Phillippians 4:7, "And the peace of God, which transcends all understanding, will guard your hearts and your minds in Christ Jesus." Jesus is our guide. He is the Way. God's ultimate gift of grace shining in the life of Jesus is our path through the tangles of life. He is our way toward our salvation. And He is our promise for a life in that same indescribable peace with God in His heaven. God's grace, shown to us in Jesus Christ, guides us.

In the final days of Advent, the flickering flame of peace whispers to us to seek God's grace. Look into the manger and see God's kindness in the gift of His son even though we do not deserve such a gift. Know this gift was given in His uncontainable love for us. We should give like that. Peek into the temple in Jerusalem where Jesus stayed behind when he was only twelve and witness His enrapt eagerness to learn His Father's teachings. We should learn like that. Immerse yourself in His parables and His miracles and experience His desire for you to understand and follow Him. We should live like that. Embrace the peace He offers when we trust Him and look ahead to the hope we have because we believe.

2 Thessalonians 3:16

> *Now may the Lord of Peace himself give you peace at all times and in every way. The Lord be with all of you.*

The Gifts of Peace

Wrapped up in swaddling clothes in a humble manger was an invitation to each of us for a one-to-one relationship with the God that loves us so tremendously. That relationship calms us, guides us and anchors us to God's infinite love and washes over us with His peace. The gift lasts forever and is always available. God wants us with Him, and He always will.

Christmas is here. Peace has been whispered down from heaven to us in the birth of Jesus. Allow His breath of peace to saturate your senses. Feel His presence as you reflect on the verses. Write down His whispers to you.

A Compassionate Gift

Luke 2:14
Romans 5:1

◆ ◆ ◆

A Calming Gift

Zechariah 9:9-10
John 12:14-15
Isaiah 43:1

◆ ◆ ◆

An Anchored Gift

Colossians 3:15
John 16:33

An Infinite Gift

Isaiah 9:6-7
Matthew 6:33

◆ ◆ ◆

A Guiding Gift

Titus 2:11-14
2 Thessalonians 3:16

Sent in a tiny, human package, God's grace brought to us Hope, Love, Joy and Peace. The Advent gifts. Gifts never to fade or disappear, these gifts are ours for eternity. Every day. Once you've unwrapped these precious gifts for yourself, your life has been enriched beyond the understanding of the world. Embrace them. Use them. Lean on them. They are the essence of God He gives to you until you meet him in Heaven. Merry Christmas!

Made in the USA
Columbia, SC
06 October 2020